Elegant Sayings

Elegant Sayings

The Staff of Wisdom
Lugs kyi bstan-bcos shes-rab sdong-po
by Nagarjuna

A Precious Treasury of Elegant Sayings
Legs-bshad rin-po-che'i gter
by Sakya Pandit

DHARMA PUBLISHING

TIBETAN TRANSLATION SERIES

1. *Calm and Clear*
2. *The Legend of the Great Stupa*
3. *Mind in Buddhist Psychology*
4. *Golden Zephyr*
5. *Kindly Bent to Ease Us*
6. *Elegant Sayings*
7. *The Life and Liberation of Padmasambhava*
8. *Buddha's Lions: Lives of the 84 Siddhas*
9. *Voice of the Buddha: Beauty of Compassion*
10. *The Marvelous Companion: Āryaśūra's Jātakamālā*
11. *Mother of Knowledge*
12. *The Dhammapada*
13. *The Fortunate Aeon (Bhadrakalpika Sūtra)*
14. *Master of Wisdom: Writings of Nāgārjuna*
15. *Joy For the World (Candragomin's Lokānanda)*

Library of Congress Cataloging in Publication Data

Nāgārjuna.
Elegant sayings.

(Tibetan translation series)
1. Proverbs, Tibetan. I. Nāgārjuna, Siddha.
Nītiśāstraprajñādanda. II. Sa-skya paṇḍita
Kun-dga'-rgyal-mtshan, 1182–1251. Subhāsitaratnanidhi.
III. Series.
PN6519.T55E4   398.9'9541   7–23433
ISBN 0–913546–12–7   ISBN 0–913546–13–5 pbk.

Frontispiece: Nāgārjuna

Typeset in Fototronic Plantin and printed by Dharma Press

10 9 8 7 6 5 4

Foreword

I felt that publishing these Elegant Sayings, which express in clear, simple language ways to lead a healthier and more spiritual life, would be of benefit to English-speaking students of Buddhism. Since these verses were written in a time and place remote from our own, their imagery may not always match our modern way of life. Still, these sayings clearly express universal truths that are meaningful and uplifting for our times. Committed to memory, and reflected upon from time to time, these verses by two outstanding masters may help ease confusion today as in centuries past.

Nāgārjuna, who lived in India probably between the first century B.C. and the first century A.D., is most widely known for his philosophical writings that set forth the Mahāyāna view and path. Sakya Paṇḍita (1182 – 1251 A.D. was an excellent Tibetan scholar, skilled in the art of literary expression. Along with Tsongkhapa and Longchenpa, he is recognized as a Mañjuśrī incarnation.

I hope this short book, dedicated to American students of Buddhism, will promote balance and harmony in your life, and encourage you to look more deeply into the vast treasury of the Dharma teachings.

Nyingma Institute　　　　　　　　　　Tarthang Tulku
Berkeley, California

The Staff of Wisdom

Harmful people should be tamed;
The wise should be reverenced.
Fill your treasury with honest deeds,
And protect your fellow men.

If you guard as your own child
Both yours and others' secrets,
All earthly things become equal
And love for man your principal affection.

3

If your spouse is untrue and your friend untrue,
If your king is untrue and your relatives as well,
If your neighbor and your country are also corrupt,
Abandon them for a distant land.

Avoid a friend who is greedy for wealth;
Avoid a partner who is fond of fornication;
Avoid a doctor who is unskilled
In curing disease.

Though you may know good from bad,
Proceed only after consultation.
If you but partially succeed,
You are yet to be admired.

Those who speak with discretion
Are respected by mankind,
As the sun, emerging from the shadows,   4
By its rays creates great warmth.

In practicing the Dharma, though you
    may suffer,
Let not your mind be anxious.
When the moon has been eclipsed,
Will it not freely shine again?

Just as for altar garlands
Only full-blown flowers are gathered,
So a gardener does not
Prematurely uproot the plant.

Rewards and royal favors,
A prostitute and a pupil's praise,
The hire of a boat and the rent of a dwelling—
These six are easily obtained.

A magic spell misunderstood is poison.
Indifference to illness is poison.
An old man with young women is poison.
A poor man's sleep in the daytime is poison.

If a worthy man who does not make
    many promises
Makes a promise under pressure,
It is like a carving on stone:
Even should he die, it is not altered.

On occasion you will come to terms
    with your enemy,
And on occasion you will quarrel
    with your friend.
Having learned to distinguish what
    should be done and what not,
The clever man selects his
    opportunity.

If your speech is careless, you will be caught
Like the parrot, the singing bird, and the
    waterhen.
The skill of the water duck,
Which man does not catch, is in keeping silent.

By keeping your weapons in order,
  your enemy will be subjugated.
By wearing poor clothes a woman's vanity
  will be subdued.
By treatment illness will be stemmed.
By effort ignorance will be swept away.

Keep your resolves to yourself,
Like a jewel which lies hidden in mud.
If its sprouts did not attract attention,
Who would find the lotus root?

Although one perceives non-existent reality,
Who can believe in its non-existence?
How could a painted peacock
Devour real pearls?

If one is plotting evil,
He always uses pleasant words.
When a hunter sees the game,
He sings a sweet song to lure it.

Whatever your intention,
Impress it clearly on men's minds:
Thus are they brought under control
As if by a wish-fulfilling gem.

It is easy to live by carrying the loads of others.
It is easy to dress in tree-bark in the forest.
It is easier for men to die
Than to spend their days in quarreling.

The nature of man is to promote harmony.
Of what value is wealth gained by contention?
Of what use is wealth and life   7
Obtained by pride and violence?

He who undertakes work he cannot complete,
Who shares views with the multitude and
    disputes with the powerful,
Who babbles his thoughts to others—
The Lord of Death sits at his door.

Look not to an evil ruler;
Look not to deceitful relatives;
Look not to a lustful partner;
Look not to a doer of harm.

Why should a man who can go anywhere
Be injured through attachment to his
    native land?
A stupid man says, "This is my own well,"
And saying thus, drinks brackish water.

A highly learned man
Has two sources of happiness—
Either he abandons all earthly interests
Or else he possesses much which could
    be abandoned.

A holy man whose glory has left him
And whose efforts have become meaningless,   8
Having become thus impoverished,
Is unhappy except in a forest.

The career of a sage is of two kinds:
He is either honored by all in the world,
Like a flower waving its head,
Or else he disappears into the silent forest.

Life, which perishes in a moment,
Has as its essence
Exhaustion and want of development.
Therefore, remain modest in the midst of it all.

An anthill increases by accumulation.
Medicine is consumed by distribution.
That which is feared lessens by association.
This is *the* thing to understand.

An anthill and understanding the teaching,
The waxing moon, 'til full,
The possessions of kings and beggars—
These increase by gradual accumulation.

Do not be excessively covetous,
For greed leads eventually to pain.
One who is led by greed is like the fox
Who was killed by the poisonous arrow
    when trying to devour the bow.

He who pursues people for what they
    can give,
And yet pays no heed to those who have
    offered much,
Is like the man who thinks only of the
    butter to come,
And pays no heed to what has already
    been churned.

Do not rely on the opinions of others
    or seek excessive fame;
Rather, look carefully and judge
    for yourself.
Be not like the forest animals
    who quickly flee
At the first cry of one frightened
    by the dropping of fruit.

Do not hurt the feelings of others
Or speak in an injurious way.
The good man and the armed enemy
Each become known.

Even if the son of his enemy speaks sweetly,
The wise man remains on guard.
A poisonous leaf retains its potency,   10
And can cause injury at any time.

Whoever benefits his enemy
With straightforward intention—
That man's enemies will soon
Fold their hands in devotion.

In desiring to injure your enemy,
Praise his inherent good qualities.
Do evil thoughts of retaliation
Injure oneself or one's enemy?

Be firm rather than mild.
Temper the unruly with suitable strength—
If the children are not diligent,
The beneficent father threatens punishment.

As long as you watch the way,
As long as your steps are steady,
As long as your wisdom is unimpaired—
So long will you reap profit.

If you always seek your own advantage,
What is the use of remaining among men?
A selfish man frustrates every chance
To make all beings rejoice.

To seek from others and yet wish for good food,
To spend your life in begging and yet have
    great pride,
To be ignorant of literary works and yet wish
    to dispute—
These three make you ridiculous to others.

The fire which burned the forest
Became the companion of the wind.
But just as the wind extinguished the fire,
The weak man loses his friends.

Not doing harm to others,
Not bowing down to the ignoble,
Not abandoning the path of virtue—
These are small points, but of great
    importance.

Having no fear of disease,
Endeavoring to associate with the wise,
Not using the language of the vulgar—
A day spent thus is greater than a
    hundred years.

Whenever the mean find a little wealth,
They despise others and are filled
    with pride.
But the virtuous, though they prosper,
Remain bowed like tall grass.

When the lowly become wealthy or learned,
They think only of quarreling with others,
Like the fox who fell into a vat of indigo
And claimed to be a tiger.

When possessed of wealth or learning,
Low people become proud.
But even when doubly honored,
The wise become more humble.

Despising to beg even though poor, delighting
      in lustful action,
Trading without profit, quarreling with leaders,
Using rough language to young women—
These five are improper conduct in a man.

The peacock, though scorched by the heat
      in the summer,
Would rather stand proudly and hope for rain
Than bend its neck
To the muddy water of the pond.

A proud bird preserves its own life
By living on dew drops,
For it fears being placed under
      obligation
And will not beg even from the gods.

If you understand Truth, why have a teacher?
When the disease is cured, why call
      a doctor?
After the water is crossed, what use is
      a boatman?
To a man without passions, what use is
      a sorcerer?

As long as a wicked man is weak—
That long is he naturally good;
Like the waters of a river in autumn
Which can be easily crossed by everyone.

If anything is much discussed,
All boast of their skill,
And as all wish to be placed foremost,
That gathering produces nothing.

14

Copulation or sleeping by day,
Fresh beer, curds, and young people drinking,
Sleeping with withered old men or women—
These six waste bodily strength.

He whose anger causes no fear,
Who can confer no benefit when pleased,
Who can neither destroy nor subjugate—
What good is such a man's anger?

Encounter with misfortune and disease,
A time of famine, danger from one's foes,
Being at the king's gate or in Yama's home—
These affect all alike.

Because of desire, people strive for worldly things
Which are neither fitting nor right.
The calf, when the milk is exhausted,
Leaves its mother at a distance.

To be separated from the object of affection,
    to be much in debt,
To have contempt for one's own people,
    to associate with evil,
To be abandoned by friends who see one's
    poverty—
These five are not fire, yet still they burn.

He who does not attempt to make peace
When small discords arise,
Is like the bee's hive which leaks drops
    of honey—
Soon, the whole hive collapses.

He who has knowledge is firm.
The holy, though destitute, do not discard
    moral virtue.
Although scorched by the sun's rays,
The natural cold of snow remains.

Those blinded by desire do not perceive
   their offense.
The blind man does not see conventional shapes.
The proud do not perceive their faults.
The egotist does not perceive the Truth.

A conqueror, a water channel,
   a creeping plant,
A person motivated by grasping,
   and a blind man—
These five are led by the crafty
When placed in the power of others.

16

The misery which follows pleasure
Is the pleasure which follows misery.
The happiness and misery of mankind
Revolve like a wheel.

The invisible appears before you
And again becomes invisible.
What of it can you hold as yours?
And how could the invisible be the
   source of pain?

The logs of wood which move
    down the river together
Are driven apart by every wave.
Why should such inevitable parting
Be the cause of misery?

The wise conquer by strength, rather than anger.
The malevolent fail by their own rage.   17
How could such men as these
Join the society of the wise?

With great effort, a large stone
May be thrown to the top of a hill,
But with little effort it may be toppled over.
Our own faults and virtues are like this.

The man who meddles in matters
Which are none of his business
Will surely come to grief,
Like a monkey which only causes confusion.

He who forsakes his own interests
And interferes in those of others
Will surely be destroyed,
Like a king who abandons his kingdom.

An astrologer makes calculations and
    divinations
Concerning the motion of the moon and stars
But he does not divine that in his own home
His woman, being at variance, is
    misbehaving.

Mistaking the moon's reflection   18
    in the still water,
You wished to seize the lotus root.
Oh, swan, who knew how to separate
    milk from water,
What has become of your knowledge today?

Any man who strives to do his best—
Whether his work be great or small—
Is considered to be doing
The work of a lion.

A ruler should not rely on his subjects
To protect his kingdom
Or overcome his plotting rivals,
But should personally attend to each
    situation.

He who says to himself, "who is the loved one
    and who the other,"
Who acts affectionately, magnanimously
And broadmindedly—such a man
Controls the whole earthly globe.

By always speaking pleasantly,
It is easy for a ruler to beguile his people.
As regards profitable words which are like
    medicine,
The speaker is rarer than the listener.

If you understand the meaning of
    the teachers
It is best to let your own conviction
    be your guide,
As when the beam of a balance is faulty
    when weighing,
Even though constructed by a
    noted craftsman.

A follower whose wealth is equal
    to his ability
And who both sees the essence of situations
    and works resolutely,
Is sure to cause you injury
As no enemy can.

If water be set on fire,
How is it to be extinguished?
If fear comes from the protector,
Who will protect from fear?

A drum, when not tuned, gives forth
    unpleasant sounds.
And even when tuned, the sound may not   20
    be sweet.
The world is like a drum;
It should be so tuned as to give forth
    a melodious sound.

A lord of the world, in passionate desire,
    does not discriminate benefit and injury.
He acts as he pleases, like a maddened
    elephant.
Tortured by remorse, he plummets over the
    precipice of despondency.
He blames others and ignores his own faults.

A king, in time of dispute,
Should preserve his life by abandoning
    his wealth—
Just as when the sheep-shearer clips
    the fleece,
The sheep thinks his spared life
    a great gain.

When there is a snake at the root
  and an eagle above,
Monkeys climbing in the branches
  and flowers surrounded by bees,
And when savage animals rest peacefully
  under its branches,
Then beware of such a sweet-smelling
  sandalwood tree.

Method is more important than strength,
When you wish to control your enemies.
By dropping golden beads near a snake,
  a crow once managed
To have a passer-by kill the snake
  for the beads.

He who has understanding is mighty;
Of what use is strength without understanding?
The hare killed the lion by wisely suggesting
That he look at his reflection in the well.

If you want to learn proper methods
  for your work,
Consult those who understand them.
With good methods your work will look
  well-done,
Even if you fail in gaining
  happiness or wealth.

The conduct of the virtuous is self-evident,
But how can it cure those who do harm?
Phlegm, which is brought on by hot spices,
Is only increased by their use.

The man against whom you feel anger
    in your heart
Is not to be admonished by mere words.
First, subdue him by force,
And then use your weapon of words.

When no danger has been encountered,
No danger is to be feared.
At a time of real danger, fear should be
    vanquished,
Like a mistake which is acknowledged.

When young, rejoice in the tranquillity
    of the old.
However great your glory, be forbearing
    in your manner.
Boast not of what you know, even when
    learned.
However high you may rise, be not proud.

Those who delight in benefiting others
Are supreme like a lamp made of a
    light-giving jewel—
It relies not on oil, nor vessel nor wick,
And yet gives forth great light.

A doctor taking food and not digesting it,
A king speaking falsehoods, and
A man of good birth misbehaving himself—
These three are very unbecoming.

By association with the exalted,
Who would not become uplifted?
The thread which strings the flowers
Becomes a garland for the head.

He who preaches at the timely season
And speaks when opportunity arises
Will be very well regarded,
And will obtain worldly greatness.

He who possesses diligence, courage,
Might, wisdom, perseverance, and
The power to subdue others
Is feared even by the gods.

Trust not your defeated enemy,
Even though he wishes to become your friend.
A raven once lit a fire in a cave
To burn the owls who were gathered there.

In eating, sleeping, fearing, and copulating,
Men and beasts are alike.
Man excels the beast by engaging
    in spiritual practice.
So, without religion, would not man be
    equal to a beast?

Those who speak ill of the spiritual life,
Although they come and go by day,
Are like the smith's bellows:
They take breath but are not alive.

One who leaves the patron, Buddha,
And bows to other gods
Is like a fool who, being thirsty,
Sinks a well on the bank of a lake.

Although you may remain in a country
    for a long time,
It is certain that you will have to leave;
Whatever may be the manner of parting,
The actual going cannot be avoided.

Compulsory separation
Brings excessive pain to the mind.
In giving up voluntarily,
Infinite peace and happiness descends.

One's desire to be attractive and happy
And to enjoy the pleasures of wealth,
Is like the foolishness of a drunken person,   25
Who, though healthy, must be carried.

There is no moral defilement equal to lust.
Nothing injures others like envy.
None is so fawning as a beggar.
There is no friend like generosity.

There is no eye like that of wisdom.
There is no night like spiritual darkness.
There is no enemy like disease.
There is no danger equal to death.

The worst of man's afflictions
Is death, which will surely come.
Therefore, turn your mind from desire
And rejoice in the Holy Dharma.

Generosity is the best friend,
And the Dharma is the most precious gem.
When common topaz is valued highly,
This will cause the ruin of the world.

Whatever there be on the surface of earth—
Property, gold, cattle, good health—
None of these truly satisfy man.
Tranquillity arises from this
    understanding.

26

Wealth, hoarded with great pains
And brought out and admired at times,
Resembles the starving mouse who hoards
    his store—
Such wealth is only a source of misery.

Earthly life is not stable;
Wealth and enjoyment never last.
Wife and child will not endure,
So trust in the Dharma and follow its teachings.

A king is not satisfied with riches, nor the
    ocean with water.
Fire is not satisfied with wood, nor the
    wise with elegant sayings.
The world can never be filled with enough
    beauty,
Nor is it possible to satisfy a child's desires.

Moral conduct, self-restraint,
And control of the mind—
What else does one need
Who perseveres in these?

If you remain utterly content,
You may easily escape the grasp of harm.
Pleasures entwined by desire
Beget trouble at every step.

This body, full of faults,
Has yet one great quality:
Whatever it encounters in this temporal life
Depends upon one's actions.

The elephant is powerful, though he
    lives on grass.
The serpent, though he lives on air, is not lean.
The ascetic, who has only a little grain and
    fruit, has his needs fulfilled.
Thus modesty and contentment are enough.

Where is the solitary retreat,
With fresh water and no overgrowth?
Even the moon is a public light,
So what is the use of claiming
    something as 'yours'?

The safest possession is contentment.
It is not difficult to earn your livelihood
Where there are fruit, leaves, and water.
Nowhere are these not found.

The lion is king of the forest, and the
    elephant the master.
Let the grass provide your cushion,
    the tree-bark your garments,
The fruit trees your food.
For whom does this impoverished society provide
    a worthy life?

Of what attractions is wealth to one
Who keeps his body pure—
And adapts himself to what he has
In situations of good or bad?

With the great price of good actions,
The ship of this body has been brought.
So long as it is not wrecked,   29
Strive to cross the ocean of misery.

As long as the moon of prosperity
    is waxing,
And as long as Death does not
    knock at your door,
Continue to live chastely,
And let your actions benefit all.

When your eyes are fixed in the stare of
    unconsciousness,
And your throat coughs the last
    gasping breath—
As one dragged in the dark to a great precipice—
What assistance are a wife and child?

Even one whose passions are controlled
    and who rejoices at the happiness of others,
Who lives simply in the woods
    and pays homage to the Buddha,
Will someday have to discard his human body.
Salvation cannot be found through books
    or through freedom from bodily suffering.

30

If thoughts are controlled by wisdom,
Then liberation is very near.
To destroy the contamination of evil,
Of what use is shaving the head?

Wealth is not proper when
Acquired through great misery,
Through acts contrary to religion,
Or through bending before an enemy.

He who does not distinguish between proper
    and improper,
Who has abandoned all heed and observance
    of religion,
Who only wishes to be filled with good food—
What difference is there between such a man
    and a beast?

Fear of being decried by society causes misery
To the holy man who longs to act nobly.
The shameless man who acts perversely,
Not caring about the proper and
     improper, is often happier.

The greatest source of virtue,
Both visible and invisible, is right knowledge.   31
Therefore, if you strive for virtue,
Take hold of wisdom in its entirety.

A hero is born among a hundred,
A wise man is found among a thousand,
But an accomplished one might not be found
Even among a hundred thousand men.

Knowledge is acquired by the wise,
Even in their old age.
Although in this life there may be no result,
In the future, good karma will surely come.

Even when one is white-haired and wrinkled,
Learning from others should be treasured.
Wherever the man of much learning may go,
He will never be overcome.

A king and an accomplished man
Are not alike.
A king is esteemed in his own country,
But an accomplished man is esteemed
   everywhere.

If an accomplished man has faults,
Philosophers do not grieve.   32
Although the moon may be obscured,
The wise look on it with pleasure.

There is no ornament like virtue,
There is no misery like worry,
There is no protection like patience,
There is no friend equal to generosity.

Though a holy man may live far away,
His virtues act as messengers.
By smelling the scent of flowers,
Bees are naturally drawn to them.

If you are truly persevering in virtue,
What is the place of a haughty attitude?
The cow which has no milk will not be
   purchased,
Even though equipped with a
   pleasant-sounding bell.

Our existence is short, the sciences are many.
We may estimate our life-span, but we do
    not know its duration.
Just as the swan separates milk from water,
Devote yourself totally to whatever you
    undertake.

Though countless stars illumine the night
And the moon brightly ornaments the earth,
Only the sun provides light for the day
And gives meaning to the terms 'east' and 'west'.

The light of the sun dispels darkness
Wherever its rays extend.
Overshadowing all other stars,
It gives supreme light to the earth.

The man who accomplishes completely
    one single act
Excels all sentient beings.
The moon when full illumines the earth—
The multitude of stars have not this power.

The growth of moral virtues depends
    upon one's self;
The acquisition of property depends upon
    previous merit.
One may be mean or poor—
Why blame others for this?

Virtues are acquired through endeavor,
Which rests wholly upon yourself.
So, to praise others for their virtues
Can but encourage one's own efforts.

Many who understand the meaning of the
    scriptures
Are among the crippled.
It is a cause of rejoicing to find the
    sharp-pointed sword
By which the enemy is conquered.

Rich men are found among barbarians,
Many heroes among the beasts.
But holy men who can explain the truth—
These are the rarest of all.

Sandalwood trees do not grow on every hill,
And pearls do not come from elephants.
The learned who can explain the
    meaning of Truth
Are not found everywhere.

True knowledge is a virtue of the talented,
But harmful to those without discernment.
Spring water free of impurity,
Entering the ocean, becomes undrinkable.

The cultured delight in culture,
But the uncultured find no pleasure there.
The bees are attracted from the forest
    by the lotus,
But the frogs of the pond never notice it.

The fame of the sagacious,
Valuables belonging to experts,
Heroes in battle—
These increase among their own kind.

The swan does not belong among hawks,
Nor the horse among donkeys,
Nor the lion among foxes,
Nor a clever man among fools.

That which the great respect
May be considered base by the vulgar,
As a stupa to which the learned bow
Is used as a seat by the crow.

Though possessing great virtue themselves,
Holy men praise accomplishments of others,
While never proclaiming their own.   36
How remarkable is such noble conduct!

The virtues of the omniscient
Are comprehended only by those who know all.
The exact weight of the earth
Is known only to the serpent-god who supports it.

If people mutually advertise each
    other's virtues,
Even he who possesses none will acquire some.
But he who proclaims his own,
Even though king of the gods, is
    not respected.

Why should a learned man
Traverse lands where learning is not respected?
What employment could a laundryman find
In a city of naked yogis?

Alas, this stupid world
Has not inspired personal initiative.
But imitating the doings of others
Is lost as metal in molten metal.

The fool prefers a buffoon to a learned man
Because he delights in laughter.
The buffoon acquires wealth
While the learned man goes empty-handed.

The sage passes his time
In beneficial spiritual practices.
By wasting this precious opportunity
    even on sleep,
Ill consequences may arise.

He who makes no effort
To acquire the virtues of the holy,
And is frightened away at seeing his own
    mother's pain—
Of what value is it for him to be born into this
    opportunity?

The way of a wise man is knowledge,
The way of the cuckoo is a sweet note,
The way of the ascetic is patience,
The way of the ignorant is perversity.

The real meaning of the Dharma and of the
    sciences
And the essence of the holy mantras
Must be directly experienced.
Do not analyze merely the meaning of the words.

When the time of need arrives,
Knowledge contained in books   38
And wealth borrowed from others
Are neither knowledge nor wealth.

The accomplishments of a teacher of ants
Are but accomplishments for earning a living.
But the study of the termination of earthly
    incarnation—
Why should that not be *the* accomplishment?

Chosen truths should not be given
To any man without due scrutiny.
Once, a man was made homeless
By giving only a small place to a monkey.

Some teach, relying on words;
Others instruct without speaking.
The reed-flower has no fruit;
The walnut has both fruit and flower.

The fruit of the kataka tree
Clears the mud from water,
But if only its name is mentioned,
The mud will not subside.

Though a man be learned,
If he does not apply his knowledge,
He resembles the blind man,
Who, lamp in hand, cannot see the road.

The clever, the disciplined,
The contented and the truthful—
It is better for such to die
Than to share a kingdom with the wicked.

In having recourse to the holy or impious,
Like the moon which waxes or wanes,
A little virtue may be increased
Or vast accomplishments may topple.

It is easier to have a learned man for
    one's enemy
Than to be friends with the stupid,
As the Brahmin who found no protection
    from the thief,
Or the king who was blinded by the monkey.

It is better to die learned,   40
Disciplined, contented, and truthful
Than to live in a kingdom
That is pervaded by wickedness.

Concerning a snake's venom and that
    of an evil man—
An evil man is more venomous than the snake,
For the snake's venom may be neutralized
    by drugs,
But what can counteract the venom of an
    evil man?

Although those who are wicked may have
    many talents,
They speak vulgar language, even when happy.
He who is learned is firm and dependable—
Although he becomes poor, he will not
    abandon virtue.

The naturally wicked man is shifty
Like the scales of a balance—
A little thing sends him up,
A little thing sends him down.

Although smeared with sandalwood, musk,
    and camphor,
The natural strong smell of garlic is not
    easily driven out.
Although many texts may be well studied,
One does not easily drive out the faults
    in one's disposition.

41

Lotuses do not grow on the face
    of a sage's son,
Nor do horns grow on the head
    of a prostitute's son.
But insofar as there was perversion in the act,
The result will be a bastard.

The words which are uttered may be different
Than the thoughts harbored in the mind.
Alas, then, for the crooked-minded!
Who can change their natural disposition?

In retaining vice and discarding virtue,
The wicked man resembles a strainer.
He assiduously retains his vices
And ever discards the moral virtues.

He who has been refuted by a wicked man
Loses confidence even in the holy.
When a child's mouth has been scalded
    by hot milk,
He drinks curds only after blowing on them.

Seeing the stars' reflection on the lake
    by night,
The swan is disappointed, mistaking them
    for lotus shoots.
So, even seeing a real lotus shoot by day,
    he will not eat it.
When once deceived by a liar, one will
    doubt even the truthful.

The appetite of one led by emotions is
    twice that of the wise;
His deceitfulness is four times,
His shame six times,
And his passions eight times as great.

Not by gifts nor by attention,
Not by worship nor by veneration,
Not by constant association nor by assiduity—
Can one led by passion be controlled.

When carried off by the King of the Birds,
The White Lotus Serpent God said:
"He who tells secrets to others
Loses his life soon after."

Just as those who steal another's husband or wife
Become the cause of all mischief,
Those who destroy one's goal and religion
Create an obstacle to the attainment
    of liberation.

If even one verse of truth
Is given by a Lama to his student,
This gift would be supreme.
A gift such as this exists nowhere on earth.

All desires should be abandoned;
But if you are unable to do so,
Let your desire be for salvation.
Thus will be found the cure.

The unhelpful relative is like a stranger,
But he who helps, though an outsider,
   is part of the family—
Like the body struck by disease
Which receives the beneficial medicine
   of solitude.

If you hold on your head attentively
A pot half-full of water,
The overflow will be as the anger
Of an evil man who is being respected.

Whatever is agreeable to your mind,
Although distant, is near.
That which is not kept firmly in mind,
Although by your side, is far away.

Though we may live together in society,
Like the water and the lotus there is no intimacy
Though sages may live far apart,
Like the moon and the lily, they admire each
   other at a distance.

Making bets, transacting money and business,
And speaking confidentially to women
Are three things to be avoided
By those desiring friendship.

When milk issues from a horn,
When the reed-flower produces honey,
When the lotus grows in dry ground,   45
Then will the deceitful speak truth.

A man of little virtue
Does not know how to use his wealth.
Like a thirsty dog that licks a glacier,
But cannot melt the ice.

Merchants and traders would not
     carry provisions
For a journey without proper payment;
But the poor, without being noticed,
Amass a hundredfold profit for the future.

Men give alms, since when we die
We leave our wealth behind.
It is wise economy to give alms, knowing that
     when we pass,
Our actions, like our property, abide.

Fearing impoverishment
The miserly never give alms.
But the learned man, knowing the danger
    of wealth,
Distributes his possessions to all.

Why not give half your food to the needy?
The desire and the reward
Which charity brings
Will be abundantly repaid in the future.

Be not grieved, though you see no results
    from your actions,
For you can still give alms
    from what you possess.
Flowers, fruit, leaves, water, and medicines
Can be made unlimited by the power
    of mental dedication.

It is an error to own wealth
Which is neither given away nor enjoyed,
For even though it is your property,
Of what use is it to you?

This is the place for action,
The beyond, the place for results.
Whatever may be done here,
Will certainly be enjoyed there.

Why be grieved at seeing the passing
Of the wealth, rank, beauty, or health
   of others?
If you desire these,
Then look to the fruits of virtuous actions.

If you have possessions but do not share
   them with others,
What is the use of keeping them nearby?
If a tree grows a fruit which is too bitter to eat,
How can it appease someone's hunger?

Giving alms which do no harm to others
Results in pleasure which cannot be carried
   away by flood,
Nor burned by fire, nor stolen by thieves.
Such possessions will never be destroyed.

He who does not try a remedy
For the disease of going to hell—
What will he do when he reaches that place
Where there is no cure to be found?

Holy men are bitten by the snake of words
Which comes from the pit of vicious men.
In order to transmute this poison
One should drink the medicines of patience
    and of wisdom.

48

Although you may spend your life killing,
You will not exhaust all your foes.
But if you quell your own anger,
Your real enemy will be slain.

The powerful are not eager to reform,
Therefore, why exercise patience with them?
With those who are disciplined and peaceful,
What need is there for patience?

If you become angry
Merely owing to an injury,
Then why not be angry with anger,
Which destroys your goal of liberation?

He who is disturbed
At seeing the excellence of others
Will not understand even a little Truth.
Such a person destroys his own merit.

Let all hear this moral maxim
And having heard it keep it well—
Do not do unto others
What is not pleasing to yourself.

Who does not seem wise
When speaking of leaving this mortal life?
But he who can practice such non-attachment
Is considered wise among sages.

Property is unstable, and youth perishes in
    a moment.
Life itself is held in the grinning fangs
    of Death,
Yet men delay to obtain release from the world.
Alas, the conduct of mankind is surprising.

He who has a good intellect but is lazy
Will never become exalted.
He is like a youthful writer
Who records his ideas in the sand.

If all sentient beings
Could perceive their coming death,
Not even food would have flavor.
What need to mention other things?

The Lord of Death does not wait to ask
Whether your works are completed or not.
Therefore, do tomorrow's work today   50
And this evening's work this morning.

As long as you are healthy and can
    produce a harvest,
Not ruined by the hail of disease,
And as long as your mind is keen and alert,
Use wisely this auspicious occasion to
    practice the Dharma.

What are wreaths of flowers to donkeys
    and cattle?
What is delicate food to four-footed
    animals and pigs?
Light to the blind or songs to the deaf?
Of what use is religious doctrine to fools?

As long as one is not ambitious,
His accomplishments will be great.
If great ambition be entertained,
How can virtue ever be acquired?

As long as a man does not beg, even when
    the time comes,
He is considered by others as a glorious ascetic.   51
Brave, clever, high, and manly
Are the terms used for a man, until he begs.

A sage's son may suitably die soon,
And a king's son suitably live long.
For a hunter's son life and death are equally
    unsuitable,
And for the saint's son equally convenient.

Of great value are those things
That exist to increase man's understanding.
Let the elegant classics be expounded
By one who understands the doctrines.

The teachings of elegant sayings
Should be collected when one can.
For the supreme gift of words of wisdom,
Any price will be paid.

The student of science, the hero,
And every beautiful woman,
Acquire great fame,
Wherever they may go.

A man of learning and a king
Are not comparable in any way.
The king is esteemed in his own country,
The wise man wherever he goes.

Whatever benefit one may give,
The wicked man is never grateful.
But do a small service to
   a holy man,
And you may command him for life.

The doings of fools are like ripples
Which on water are quickly effaced.
Those of a holy man, though small,
Are permanent, like carvings on stone.

The evil man may speak sweetly;
Nevertheless, he is not to be trusted.
The peacock has a sweet note,
But for food it eats powerful poison.

Alas, the wicked man and
Mucus are really alike.
By gentleness they are excited
And by roughness they are soothed.

A wicked man, gold, a drum,
A wild horse, the ignorant, and cloth—
These are controlled by beating.   53
They are not vassals for elegant actions.

Association with a wicked person is unbecoming,
Whether he is pleasant or obnoxious,
Like being with a dog is unbecoming,
Whether you play with him or let him
    lick you.

Wildness is worse than a serpent.
By drugs and charms
A serpent's venom can be expelled,
But wildness cannot be banished.

The misdeeds of the undisciplined
Leave their mark on the mind.
Whoever mixes with the unruly
Becomes even more unruly than they.

Even without intention
A son imitates his father's conduct.
From a magic tree
One does not get sour fruit.

If my father, mother, brother, or wife
Imitate my actions,
Whatever sin I may commit,
It is as if they had committed it.

This earth, the mighty ocean,
And the mountains are not a burden.
But he who is ungrateful
Is indeed a heavy weight.

He who stays in the society of the moral
Rejoices in benefiting even evil beings.
Although Yama is the destroyer,
Wise men praise him very much.

In the society of the clever, the disciplined,
The contented, and the truthful,
Imprisonment is a superior state.
The sovereignty of the unruly is not thus.

He who is handsome, youthful, accomplished,
And born to a high family,
Like the blossom of the lilac tree,
Does not look well when split from his
line of descent.

He who has a body but is devoid of learning,
Though of good birth, what use is he?
In the world, reverence comes from learning;
From lack of learning, destruction proceeds.

If you desire ease, forsake learning.
If you desire learning, forsake ease.
How can a man at ease acquire knowledge,
And how can an earnest student enjoy ease?

He who is no friend of knowledge
Will always be in misery.
He who is a friend of knowledge
Will always attain to joy.

What country is foreign to a sage?
Who is hostile to a pleasant speaker?
What load is heavy to a man in his own home?
What distance too great to the strong?

Because he who is earnest has friends,
The summit of Sumeru is not too high,
The earth's depths are not too low,
The ocean cannot separate him from
　　his goals.

The man who has learned from books alone
And has not studied from many standpoints
Resembles a pregnant girl of loose morals—
He does not look well among his peers.

He who scorns the Lama
Who has given him even a single teaching
Will pass through a hundred dog-incarnations
And be reborn in a lower realm.

Sufficient wealth does not exist
To repay a Lama
Even for a single teaching
To his student.

He who imparts elegant learning,
He who teaches science, he who brings one up,
He who feeds one, and he who gives
　　fearlessness—
These five are like fathers.

The wife of a king or a minister,
Likewise, the wife of a friend,
A brother's wife, and one's own mother—
These five are like mothers.

Counsel given to fools
Excites but does not pacify.
He who pours milk for a snake
Is only increasing its venom.

The fool who acts like a two-footed beast
Should be especially avoided.
For, like the unseen thorn,
The pain of his words can go deep.

When a fool sees another fool,
He is more refreshed than by the scent of
    sandalwood.
If he sees a learned man,
He jealously accuses him of parricide.

Intimacy in the society of the holy,
Conversation in the society of the learned,
And friendship with the unselfish—
These will cause no regrets.

Although for a very long time
You may not perceive the misery
Of this world and the next,
Yet bring your mind into harmony with religion.

Although a thing may afford enjoyment,
If the result be injurious, how can
   it be right?   58
If something upsets your health,
How could it be right to eat such a dish?

That which hurts but is profitable
Is drunk by the wise like medicine.
The result, afterwards attained,
Becomes in itself incomparable.

If a learned king
Were to summarize these teachings,
In the beginning, the middle, and the end
They would not appear other than elegant.

It is said that when the ocean is no more,
We can cross it even in the middle.
Whether holy men are present or not,
We should not transgress the moral teachings.

Thus ends the Commentary on Manners
Called *The Staff of Wisdom*,
Written by Pandit Nagarjuna.   59

A Precious Treasury of
Elegant Sayings

Acquire knowledge though you may die
    next year.
Although in this life you may not become wise,
In your future birth, if taken with you,
It will become a precious thing.

If you are a talented man,
Everyone gathers around you without
    being called.
A scented flower, though far distant,
Attracts a cloud of swarming bees.

A wise man, though possessed of
    immense perfections,
Will learn from others.
By such continual practice,
He will at last become omniscient.

If a wise man behaves prudently,
How can he be overcome by his enemies?
Even a single man, by right action,
Can overcome a host of foes.

A brave, wise, and fortunate man,
Though alone, overcomes all.
The lion, the king of beasts, and
The universal monarch need no assistant.

If you are wise,
You may make a slave of the great—
As the garuda, though a strong and mighty bird,
Is made the vehicle of the god Vishnu.

The wise, when studying, suffer pains;
Without exertion, it is impossible to become wise.
He that is passionate for a small pleasure
Can never reach great peace.

If you are intelligent, though you be weak,
What can a powerful enemy do to you?
The King of the wild beasts, though strong,
Was killed by an intelligent hare.

The ocean is never too full of water.
The king's treasury is never too full of money.
One is never satisfied with enjoyment.
Wise men overflow with elegant sayings.

Even from children,
Wise men receive fine sayings.
For the sweet scent,
The navel of a musk deer must be opened.

It is always by excellent men
That good qualities are praised most.
The scent of sandalwood is diffused by the wind
Into the ten corners of the world.

If a virtuous man is chosen as Master,
Everyone will find contentment.
When a ceremony is properly performed,
It will be a benefit to all.

When men are injured by a wicked ruler,
Then will they remember a virtuous one.
They that suffer a malignant fever
Think only of cool water.

When a wicked prince does injury,
A virtuous king is ready to defend him.
He who is occupied by an evil spirit
Is cheerfully assisted by a magician.

Even in decline, a virtuous man
Increases the beauty of his behavior.
A burning stick, though turned to the ground,   66
Has its flame drawn upwards.

A virtuous prince, though far away,
Favorably protects his own followers.
When the clouds in the sky gather together,
The corn of the field increases.

During life, renown is the cause of joy.
In the world, happiness is a man's delight;
Without these two, a wise man
Can have no pleasure in wealth alone.

Excellent qualities, though not displayed,
Spread and become visible everywhere.
The blossoms of the nutmeg tree, though dried,
Diffuse their sweet scent in all directions.

A king is great only in his dominions,
While a virtuous man is respected wherever he goes;
A flower is beautiful for a day,
A gem is everywhere esteemed.

A hen at rest lays many eggs.
A peacock, when still, has a handsome tail.
A gentle horse has a swift pace.
Quietness is the sign of a sage.

Though equal benefits be conferred
On the excellent and the vulgar, the return
    is not equal.
Though there is no difference in the seed
    sown in different fields,
Yet there is immense variety in the crop.

Preserve your noble descent by your conduct—
When your practice is bad, your birth is
    of no value.
The sandalwood has a fine scent,
But when reduced to ashes, who will buy it?

The great, though sometimes distressed,
Have no reason to be grieved.
The moon, though eclipsed for a while,
Soon appears again.

If a great man treats kindly an enemy,
That very enemy comes under his sway.
The universal monarch, since he
    protected all,
Was elevated to dignity by everyone.

The holy man, though he be distressed,
Does not eat food mixed with wickedness.
The lion, though hungry,
Will not eat what is unclean.

The holy man, though it may cost him his life,
Will not desist from what is good.
The color of fine gold will not change,
Though it be burnt and broken.

Though low-minded men may be angry
    with a holy man,
How could that holy man become
    wrathful in return?
Though the jackal may utter a
    nonsense language,
The king of the forest mercifully
    protects him.

People seek to find fault
With the excellent and not with the low.
All look with awe on costly belongings,
But who would notice a fire-brand?

Not to be cheered by praise,
Not to be grieved by blame:
To know well one's own perfections   69
Is the characteristic sign of an excellent man.

Riches are not in vain
That are gained through knowledge, strength,
    and skill.
The dog and the cat, though they stand erect,
Are living examples of ignorance.

It adds to the master's greatness
If his disciples are well satisfied.
The embellishments of a horse—
Are they the master's own ornaments?

As the master takes care of
And kindly protects his disciples,
So do the disciples
Manage the master's affairs.

At the place where the great Lord Buddha
    is present,
Who would acknowledge another man?
Though there be many bright stars in the heaven,
When the sun has arisen none of them can be seen.

A wicked man, though he obtains wealth,
Grows worse in his conduct.   70
A stream, though turned back,
Endeavors to flow downwards.

Though a wicked man appears good
    in his conduct,
It is but hypocrisy.
Though a crystal be made to have the color
    of a gem,
When put in water it shows its own color.

A great man's wise arrangements
Are destroyed in a moment by wicked men.
A farmer cultivates a corn-field
    for years and months—
A hail storm suddenly destroys all effort.

A man with bad qualities
Infects others.
A crow, after eating
   something unclean,
Earnestly rubs its bill on the ground.

If one entrusts his business to a fool,
Both the fool and the business will collapse.
If a fox were elected king,
Both the fox and the king would be destroyed.

The foolish man, in wishing for happiness,
Works only toward his own distress.
Someone under an evil influence,
In wishing to be freed from pain, deprives
   himself of life.

The action of a man who cares nothing
For the welfare of others is like that
   of a beast—
Though he may attend the dinner party,
He makes no effort to prepare the food.

He that makes no reflection on what is
    useful and what is not,
And does not improve his understanding
    and experience,
Is a swine without hair
That seeks only to fill his belly.

One may boast of his wisdom among the fools,   72
But before the wise he is silent.
Though one has no hump or fur coat,
He that has fangs is a beast.

One who hastens to where there is food,
But runs away at the first sign of work—
Though he resembles a man by speaking
    and laughing,
Is more like an old dog without a tail.

It is easy to fill a beast's footstep with
    water.
A small treasury may easily be piled full
    of gold.
To sow a small field with corn requires little
    labor.
To satisfy the curious, a little knowledge
    will do.

One who makes many promises
   because of his pride,
Though he be great, will be defeated.
By promising small plots of ground,
Even the gods will eventually be defeated.

Ignorant people believe a monkey-catcher
To be greater than a wise man.
When great delicacies are served
   along with bread and meat,
They come back uneaten.

Illiterate men are sometimes more inimical
To learned men than to others.
It is said that if a cornstalk sprouts
   through the snow,
It is an unlucky omen.

Some who have little knowledge
Will find fault with those who understand.
It is counted a defect on some islands
Not to have a goiter.

They that know only imperfectly the
   religious rites
Condemn those that perform them well.
In some ancient countries, he who
   walks on two feet
Is not counted as a man.

Those who act wrongly   74
But criticize those who do right
Are like homely men who contemptuously say
That he who is handsome is merely effeminate.

Foolish men, though they be many,
Go directly into the power of the enemy.
A whole herd of strong elephants can be subdued
By one intelligent hare.

Riches without understanding
Are of little advantage,
As the cow's milk can support the calf
For but a limited time.

Foolish men who amass riches
By all manners of wickedness,
Neglecting support of even their families,
Will soon die away like rats.

He who looks always to others for support
Will most certainly fail,
As the tortoise that wanted to be
    carried by crows
Was eventually dropped to the ground.

Not to understand what is good and bad,
Not to remember a kindness one has received,
Not to marvel at what one has clearly
    perceived—
These are the characteristics of a foolish man.

When the troops are advancing, he is
    in the rear,
When they retire, he goes to the front,
Where there is food he endeavors by all
    means to partake—
Thus are the actions of a fool.

A mean fellow, though he be rich, is outdone
By a little man of noble descent.
When the hungry tiger uttered a deep sound,
The monkey fell from the treetop.

A foolish man proclaims his qualifications,
A wise man keeps them secret within.
A straw floats on the surface of water,
But a precious gem placed upon it
    sinks to the depths.

Those with little learning have great pride;
Grown wise, they are quiet.
Torrents always make much noise,
But it is seldom that the ocean roars.

It is always the low-minded men
Who speak disdainfully to the holy,
Like the foxes which attack the lion,
Though he be their defender.

The generous, though angry, are gentle when one
    bows before them.
The mean, yielded to, grow haughty.
Gold and silver, though hard, may be melted.
Dog's dung stinks when burned.

A wise man consists entirely of perfections.
A fool has only his defects.
With precious metals you may pay all
    your expenses.
From a venomous serpent expect
    nothing but distress.

A wicked man, though he abides in
    a forest, is mean.
A virtuous man, though he resides in
    a town, is serene.
We see that a wild beast of the forest
    is fierce,
But a fine horse in the town is gentle.

An excellent man reflects on his own faults alone.
A bad man seeks only those of others.
The peacock judges his own body,
But a bat casts ill omens on others.

An excellent man, by his gentleness, preserves
    both himself and others.
A bad man causes pain both to himself and
    to others by his harshness.
A fruit tree nourishes both itself and others.
A dry tree, by its stiffness, cumbers both
    itself and others.

As long as you have wealth, everyone is
    your friend;
If your fortune declines, everyone is your foe.
An island of precious metals is visited
    from afar;
When a lake dries up, everyone leaves.

It is only by narrow-minded men
That such distinctions are made as to
    friend and enemy.
A liberal man is affectionate towards all,
Since it is uncertain who may yet be
    useful to him.

Learned men delight in knowledge;
The ignorant do not.
Honey bees resort to flowers;
Not so the fly.

A learned man is beautiful among learned men.
How can the wise be understood by the fool?
See how sandal-wood that is more precious
    than gold
Is by foolish people reduced to coal.

A wise man guides his own course of action;
The fool follows another's direction.
When an old dog barks, the others run,
And this for no reason at all.

A wise man, though in decline,
Affords pleasure to others by his
    elegant sayings.
A fool, grown violent,
Destroys himself and others through
    quarreling.

Some place perfection in speaking;
Others are silent and penetrate to the meaning.
A stupid dog utters his first fear to the enemy;
A cat catches a mouse without a sound.

When a virtuous man disputes, he benefits all.
A fool causes damage even by his friendship.
Though the gods be angry, they defend
    all sentient beings.
The Lord of Death may smile, but still kills his
    enemies.

An excellent man, like precious metal,
Is in every respect invariable.
A villain, like the beam of a balance,
Is always shifting up and down.

As long as one is modest,
He is adorned with the chief quality.
When modesty is gone, good   80
    qualities decrease,
And ill rumor spreads about.

A virtuous man gives instructions
    without hypocrisy;
If you ask a villain, he will misinform you.
Though you slight a Bodhisattva, he is
    merciful,
Though you bestow praise on the Lord of Death,
    he is still your destruction.

What is helpful to one
May cause another pain,
As when the moon rises,
The evening flowers open,
    the lotuses close.

Though by wicked acts one may reach one's aim,
A wise man never resorts to such means.
The wise are not ashamed if they do not
   reach their goal,
Provided they have righteously
   endeavored for it.

It is difficult to cause dissension among
   the virtuous,
But it is easy to reconcile them.
Low people can easily be separated, but with
   difficulty reconciled.
See what a difference there is between the
   sandal-tree and the coal made of its wood.

Though a virtuous man decline for awhile,
Like the increasing moon, he rises again.
If a low man once is decayed,
He will be extinguished like a lamp.

Wealth to a low man is a cause of pride;
To a virtuous man, it is that of humbleness.
The fox, when he has filled his belly,
   behaves proudly;
The lion, when full, takes his repose.

A virtuous prince shows more
   affection to his subjects
When he finds them his enemies.
A mother is more grieved
When her child is sick.

A good person, if he associates with a bad man,
Will be infected thereby.
Pure water, though very pleasing to the taste,
When it reaches the sea, smacks of the brine.

If a low-principled man keeps company
   with a Holy man.
His manners become like those of the sage.
See what a fragrant scent the person gives off
Who has anointed himself with musk.

Mount Sumeru cannot be moved
   by any creature—
So too the excellent man stands firm.
Just as a small piece of cotton is easily moved—
So the practice of a low-minded man changes
   greatly.

As the laughing voice of the night-bird
Is an ill omen, is not born of joy,
So the gracious speech of a cunning man
Arises from self-interest.

If a successful man grows too famous,
Though he endures for a while,
   he will at last be destroyed.
The ass, covered with a leopard skin,
    may eat one field of corn
But will be slain by the farmer next door.

Those who have chosen a wicked man
   for their leader,
Or those who dwell in a house whose
   roof is decayed,
Or under a rock whose summit threatens to fall,
Are in continual fear.

If a man is by nature wicked,
Avoid him even though he is learned.
Although a venomous serpent has a gem
   on his head,
What wise man would take him into his heart?

By arrogance, good qualities are diminished.
By lust, modesty is destroyed.
By a continual railing at his disciples,
The master loses his authority.

It is rare to find one who can give good
    counsel.
It is more rare to find one who listens to advice. 84
It is difficult to find an expert physician.
Fewer still will take his medicine.

Judge not before you have examined.
It often happens that an upright man, if he
    loses his cause,
Is thought to be a knave.
He that acts with discretion has many enemies.

In whatever manner you fashion a wicked man,
It is impossible to make his nature good.
You may wash charcoal with zeal,
But you will not make it white.

An ill-principled man, who is fond of riches,
Is not of firm mind, though he may be a friend.
There are many that have been destroyed
By taking bribes from the powerful.

It is easy to overcome those enemies
That announce their plans;
But how are those to be subdued
Who advise a salutary retreat?

If we should be chosen as ruler,
It is unlikely that we would know what to do.
We may look on others with our own eyes,   85
But we need a mirror to see ourselves.

Though there are many kings,
There are few who govern with righteousness.
Though there are many gods in the heavens,
None shines brighter than the sun or the moon.

He that can do mischief
Can also do good.
A crowned monarch can rule as a tyrant
Or bestow his kingdom on another.

Under the rule of an upright,
    intelligent minister,
Both the sovereign and the subjects
    can be contented.
An arrow shot by a skillful archer
Strikes its mark.

When many work together for a goal,
Great things may be accomplished.
It is said a lion cub was killed
By a single colony of ants.

One who lacks energy and is lazy
Shall decay though he is robust and strong.
Though an elephant has much strength,
He is treated by his small driver as a slave.

Even great men can be overpowered
If their arrogance becomes too great.
Though the white tortoise is small,
He can destroy a large crocodile.

The great have no need to be arrogant,
And the arrogance of the lowly is futile.
A true gem wants no recommendation,
But a false jewel goes unwanted, though it be
    highly praised.

Men are often injured
By men similar to themselves.
At the rising of the sun,
The stars and moon disappear.

Retain those who are helpful, though
    they may be enemies.
Reject those who hurt you, though
    they may be relatives.
Buy, at whatever the price, a jewel
    brought from the sea.
Drive out, by good medicine, the disease in
    your inward parts.

When a man gains wealth within,
He shows it with pride without.
When the clouds are full of water,
They move and rumble with thunder.

It is rare to find one who is perfect,
But it is rare also to find one who has no
    good qualities.
A wise man will attend to one
Who leans more to virtue than to vice.

It may be doubtful, at first,
Whether a person is an enemy or friend.
Meat, if not properly digested, becomes poison;
But poison, if used rightly, may turn medicinal.

To be one's own master is counted as happiness.
To be in the power of others is held to be misery.
Common property is the cause of quarrels.
Promises are the cause of being bound.

You may inwardly possess good qualities,
But if dressed improperly, you will be looked
    down upon by others.
Though the bat is a prudent animal,
Since he has no feathers, he is rejected
    by all birds.

A foolish man is pleasing when he speaks
    but little.
A king is dignified when he maintains seclusion.
Imposing spectacles are impressive if viewed
    at a distance.
A rare jewel always brings a great price.

Great affection is often
The cause of violent animosity.
The quarrels of men often arise
From too great a familiarity.

It may happen sometimes that a long debate
Becomes the cause of a longer friendship.
Commonly, those who dispute with one another
At last agree.

Though an avaricious man possesses wealth,
An envious man possesses another's goods,
And an ill-minded man possesses his learning—
None of these can produce lasting pleasure.

Covetous men delight in wealth;
Ambitious men are pleased when they hear their
    own praise;
Foolish men rejoice at finding a fool;
Virtuous men rejoice at hearing the truth.

The qualifications of a wicked man,
The imperfect learning of a mighty speaker,
And the kindness of a bad master
Are seldom useful to others.

If a man is wealthy, his voice
   is easily heard.
A poor man, though he speaks the truth,
   is not listened to.
A common piece of wood, brought
   from a distant mountain,
Will bring a high price.

Much talking is the cause of danger.
Silence is the means of avoiding misfortune.
The talkative parrot is shut up in a cage.
Other birds, without speech, fly freely about.

When a man sincerely endeavors to be useful
To an enemy in every respect,
And when the enemy also yields to him without
   pretension—
These show great character.

Of what avail is a weak man's anger?
What need is there for a strong man's wrath?
So there is no need for anger,
Except to mortify oneself.

With gifts, you may gather your enemies
    about you.
When giving nothing, even your own
    family will leave.
When the cow's milk becomes dry,
The calf grows meager and wanders in sorrow.

A master who always treats his servants kindly
May easily find those who work hard.
At lakes where many lotuses blossom
The geese gather together without being called.

When one employs riches,
When one is gentle and learned,
When one protects the lower class of people—
These three make others happy and are useful
    to oneself.

By depending on the great,
The small may rise high.
See: the little plant ascending the tall tree
Has climbed to the top.

Though a talented man has his defect,
They that delight in learning support him.
Though the atmosphere is obscured by rain,
Beings are made glad by it.

Rich men are numerous among the ignorant.
Valiant ones abide alone with wild beasts.
Elegant sayings proceed from the learned.
But a Saint is rare in this world.

Every man is celebrated
For the thing in which he excels—
The sage as a learned person,
The hero as a valiant man.

What is respected by the great
Is condemned by the lowly.
The precious crown of the gods
Is devoured by the ogre.

Knowledge existing only in books,
Mantras not committed to memory,
And those things which a forgetful man
    has learned
Often deceive us in a time of necessity.

Offering sweet scents to dogs and pigs,
A light to the blind, meat to those with
indigestion,
Or instructions to the foolish—
These actions are senseless.

A talented man and good gold,
A brave soldier and a fine horse,
A skillful physician and a beautiful
ornament
Are everywhere esteemed.

If one is intelligent and applies himself well,
What can he not accomplish?
Even small bands of people, I have heard,
Have defeated whole armies.

Though hills and rivers, elephants and horses,
sunshine and storms, and men and women
Are the same according to their classes,
They can be distinguished
By being great or lowly.

The chief wealth consists in charity,
The greatest happiness is tranquillity of mind;
Experience is the most beautiful ornament,
The man without desires is the best companion.

No person exists that does not sometimes
    desire wealth.
What person is there who is always happy?
Pleasure and sorrow are always changing,
Like summer and winter.

If a slave behaves with great pride,
If the actions of an ascetic are fruitless,   94
If a ruler does not act according to moral law—
All three have taken a misguided course.

To act indiscreetly, to have rancor
    against many,
To quarrel with the powerful, to be
    passionate for women,
To cleave to what is bad—
These five are the causes of quick destruction.

When one is poor and yet desires fine garments,
When one lives on charity and yet behaves
    haughtily,
When one is ignorant of scriptures, and yet
    wishes to dispute—
These three make one a laughing-stock
    among men.

Sovereigns suffer more injury
From their own people than from enemies.
By what other animals is the corpse devoured,
Except by worms in his own body?

When a Master does evil to himself,
Who can defend him against it?
When the sun lights the sky in the daytime,   95
There is no way to see the stars.

Some malicious men, though they derive no
    direct benefit,
Like to do wrong to others.
Though a venomous serpent feeds on the air,
When he sees others, he kills them.

Though we believe our lust to cause happiness,
It is actually the root of sorrow.
He that sees happiness in drinking wine
Imagines that only mad men are happy.

Men wish to live long,
But when they grow old, are afraid of old age.
To be afraid of old age and to wish for
    long life
Is the poor logic of a foolish man.

One who has a wise teacher
But will not learn from him how to develop
   good qualities,
Either is occupied by demons,
Or is suffering the ill consequences of his
   former actions.

One who has wealth but does not enjoy it,   96
Or give it charitably to others,
Is either a very sick man
Or an accomplished miser.

One who knows what virtue is but does not
   practice it—
Of what use is his religion?
If a fine crop is harvested,
Do not even the wild beasts rejoice?

One who suffers from the ill consequences of
   his past bad actions,
Though he has riches, cannot enjoy them.
Though the crow is hungry, if a snare has
   been laid,
How can he be satisfied?

If you believe a man to be rich
Who can neither enjoy his wealth nor bestow it
   charitably on others,
It is like considering a man rich
Who fancies a mountain to be solid gold.

Though there be many learned men
Who know and proclaim what virtuous action is,   97
There are very few in this world
Who would practice it, having thus understood.

Though a man has a youthful appearance,
Without good qualities, he is not handsome.
Though a peacock's feathers are beautiful,
Are they appropriate dress for a man?

Through no amount of effort can a
   naturally wicked man
Be turned into an honest one.
However long you boil water,
It is impossible to make it burn like fire.

If there is reason, it is proper to be angry,
And there is also a cure for this anger.
But who knows how to appease
One grown angry without a cause?

When one's virtues fail, ill-will arises.
When legitimate descent is absent,
    a bastard is born.
When wealth has been depleted,
    many desires arise.
When life is spent, the symptoms of
    death appear.

If one has not committed any wicked action,
The gods cannot lay blame.
Can a spring be blocked by heaping
    earth on it
When it has not previously gone dry?

Even great minds can be led astray
If guided in an appealing manner.
Those who do not follow the Dharma
Adopt the practices of false teachers.

When a man becomes too famous for his riches,
He is destroyed by his wealth.
It is common that rich men are assaulted,
But beggars pass through without harm.

If a man becomes renowned for his
   strength and skill,
He merely proposes his own destruction.
Many of those who have been slain in battle
Have been the strong and skillful.

Wealth, wit, and strength will come to you
If you practice virtuous deeds;
But, these actions absent,
Wealth and strength will become your ruin.

A wise man, whenever he acts,
Must consider the moral effects.
Among a hundred persons, it is rare to find
Even one of accomplished moral merits.

When a broken tank is filled with water,
It certainly will leak on every side.
Weak men who grow rich
Seldom leave an inheritance.

Seldom a man has both wealth and children.
One who has both is frequently destroyed.
When one is happy in every respect,
He is often carried off by early death.

A person who is prosperous in every respect
Is one who has acquired merit.
A man who acts wisely increases his virtue,
Which alone results in prosperity.

He who thinks thus, "I will deceive him,"
Actually deceives himself.
If a person has lied even once,   100
Although later he speaks the truth, he
    will be doubted.

He who does not examine what is good and bad,
And injures his neighbor in a fit of anger,
Shall grieve like the swallow
Who loses his companion.

Apply yourself both now and in the next life.
Without effort, you cannot be prosperous.
Though the land be good,
You cannot have an abundant crop without
    cultivation.

An intelligent man must give due consideration
Even to small matters.
If he succeeds, what could be better?
And, if he fails, it is good to have
    acted prudently.

The minds of men are very different,
And it is hard to satisfy the wishes of all.
But he who is accomplished in all good qualities
Comes closest to fulfilling all desires.

Increase your wisdom, even in your
        declined age.
In the next life, it will be useful to you.
Without such wisdom,
Even your alms will be of no avail.

Either keep company with those who are
        accomplished in knowledge
Or converse with ordinary men.
You may carry a bottle with you easily,
Whether it is full or empty.

Of what use is a man
Who has acquired little knowledge?
Who would carry a water-pot on his head
When it is but half-filled?

He that understands well
The difference between an excellent and low man
Knows how to act.
This is the great foundation of prosperity.

Holding a firm resolution for perfection,
A lowly man may become great.
If a parrot is well instructed,
He can learn to distinguish value.

Men of few abilities
May succeed if they depend on the great.
A drop of water is a small thing;
United with a lake it never dries.

Though a man is not intelligent,
He may prudently consult the wise.
The hand cannot kill an enemy,
Unless it takes a weapon in firm grasp.

Even a dangerous enemy can be made
    into an ally
If the proper means are known.
A large quantity of poison harms the body,
But the right mixture of even poison
    works towards health.

Accept humbly the food and money offered
    to you for your learning.
Listen to others and leave behind pride.
You may take the fruit from the top of a tree,
But if you reach farther, you will fall.

As long as you have not sufficient strength,
Bear patiently with your enemy.
When you are strong enough,
Then do what seems to be best.

Treat with due respect
And reward liberally those around you.
It is said that with sacrifices and offerings
One receives fully from the gods as well as
    other beings.

When done correctly,
A prince may tax his subjects without
    oppressing them.
A sal-tree becomes dry
If too much fragrant juice issues from it.

Carefully conceal the manner of your actions;
Often it is a weakness to plainly show
    intentions.
Had the thief's eyes not been found devising,
Would a rope have been tied around his neck?

Of what use are food and goods
Which have been rejected by others?
What wise man would touch such dirty things
As are eaten by dogs and swine?

We should never use expressions
Which might hurt even an enemy.
They immediately will return to us
Like an echo from a rock.

If you wish to injure an enemy,
Make yourself perfect in all good qualities.
Thus, your enemy will be mortified,
And your yourself shall improve in virtue.

104

Only a fool is kind-hearted to an enemy,
After being treated harshly by him.
He who wishes to cure his body of cancer,
Must have the malignant portion removed
    with a knife.

Though our allies are angry with us, we
    should not desert them.
Though an enemy treats us with kindness,
    we should not embrace his cause.
Though a crow hurts another crow,
They do not side with an owl.

A wise man, in great or small matters,
Must act with due consideration.
Whether attacking a hare or an elephant,
The lion has no time for indecision.

By residing with excellent men,
We may profit thereby,
Like birds of Sumeru
Who shine like gold.

If you depend on a great but envious man,
You never shall obtain renown.
See how the moon declines
After coming too near the sun.

Who can associate with a man
Who keeps no friendship?
Though a rainbow is beautiful,
Only a fool would mistake it for a jewel.

What we do not like for ourselves,
We should never do for others.
When we are injured by others,
We should reflect what we think of ourselves.

If one does to others
What is agreeable to oneself,
Others, in the same manner,
Will return the kindness.

Weak-minded men think
That everything they say is wrong.
Those who think thus and speak little
Are very much suspected by others.

He is continually happy
Who has the opportunity of depending
    on the excellent,
Of consulting the learned,
And of conversing with the good-natured.

Speak only at the proper place and time,
After having given due consideration.
If you utter elegant sayings too often,
Even they lose their value.

The defects of a learned man
Are seldom taken as imperfections.
Those who confess such defects
Are often faulty men.

If it has a wise friend for a companion,
A beast can accomplish useful actions.
Even if he has no wealth or servants,
How much more could be done by a man?

We should not join with an enemy who has
    fought long against us,
Even though he wants our friendship.
If fire meets with hot water,
Will it not be extinguished?

We may rely upon an enemy
If he is good-natured, righteous, and honest.   107
I have heard that, by resorting to a good-
    tempered enemy for protection,
One has been defended by him to life's end.

Though you be well acquainted with the subject,
Do everything with due consideration.
He that neglects this
Shall dearly pay for his indiscretion.

If you resort to an enemy for protection,
Show him every respect and reverence.
The raven, by depending on a rat,
According to the *Puranas*, was saved.

How is it possible to fail in your affairs,
As long as you act with discretion?
If a clear-sighted man walks discreetly,
Will he not avoid the precipice?

The more you desire to be exalted,
The more you should endeavor to be useful
    to others.
Those who wish to apply make-up
First clean the looking-glass.

If you endeavor to conquer an enemy,
Exert all your good qualities.
See how they are confounded
Who watch their enemy prepare his weapons.

It is impossible in this world
To obtain your wish through abuse.
Though selfish in your mind,
Be affable to all in speaking.

Using harsh and gentle means matters not
If our concern be for the welfare of others.
The Buddha has not called it craftiness
To employ wise means in our actions.

When a prudent man hangs down his head,
The fault falls on the one who abuses.
When a candle is held downwards,
It burns the hand of the holder.

Each thing should be placed
According to its proper use.
A hat is not worn on the feet,
And shoes do not make good hats.

When doing important work,
Find a good associate.
If you wish to burn a forest,
You need the aid of the wind.

Do not be grieved if you are poor,
Or be elated with joy if you are rich.
Rather, consider the consequences
Of your deeds.

One who pays homage to another teacher
When the Buddha, patron of men,
    lives near,
Is like a man who digs a well
On the bank of a clear-flowing river.

Actions to which we are well accustomed
Pose no difficulty.
As we have learned well our worldly skills,
So we may practice virtues without difficulty.

For a man who is contented with little,
Wealth is inexhaustible.
He who continually seeks and is never satisfied
Will experience a constant rain of sorrow.

Give the goods you have received
To others according to their need.
Like the bee's honey,   110
All hoarded treasures are eventually
    enjoyed by others.

If you lend money, it is uncertain
Whether you shall be repaid;
But if you bestow alms, though they be small,
Your return will be a hundred-fold.

Fearing his family's impoverishment,
A narrow-minded man anxiously hoards
    what little he has.
A wise man, hoping for a good position,
Bestows his alms on others, like bribes.

Though children are loved by their parents,
They do not return love with respect.
After parents have long cherished
    their children,
They are despised when they grow old.

Those who have become the slaves of the world
Run after riches at the price of destruction.
The wise man, though he obtains wealth,
Is contented to give it to others.

If you would fight an enemy who harms you,
Then subdue your own passions.
Thus, you shall be perfectly free from harm;　　　111
For it is on account of your passions that
From the beginning you have been wandering
　　in the world.

If you wish to destroy all your enemies,
You never shall find the end of killing.
But if you can subdue your own desire,
Every enemy is at once destroyed.

If you are angry with powerful and malicious men,
You will only hurt yourself.
What reason is there to be angry
With the virtuous and the wise?

Herbs which grow in the same garden
Are dispersed by the wind in the ten
　　directions.
Men who are born together
Are separated by the effects of their deeds.

If you earnestly desire your own welfare,
First seek that of others.
He that seeks only his own benefit
Will not succeed in his purpose.

A foolish man who will not learn
    believes everything a miracle.
A wise man, having studied, admires all,
And, though grown old,
Acquires knowledge for his future birth.

The fool seeks not to acquire knowledge,
Having no mind for understanding.
For this very reason, he should endeavor
To improve his understanding.

One that has not gained knowledge in his former birth
Is ignorant in the present life.
He who fears ignorance in his next life,
Must study assiduously in this one.

"Meditate! There is no need to learn by
    instructions,"
Says the shallow-minded fool.
Contemplation without previous instruction,
Though diligently pursued, is the way of
    the beast.

It is by the perfection of wisdom
That omniscience differs from common
    knowledge.
How would this infallible doctrine be true,
If, without learning, one could become
    all-knowing?

Meditation without hearing,
Though it succeeds for a while, will soon fail.
You may melt gold and silver,
But, taken from the fire, they
    harden anew.

Though a literary work is excellent,
He that lacks understanding will not
    appreciate it.
Though an ornament of gold beset
    with jewels is beautiful,
Would an ox look closely upon it?

Know well what is true—
That which is expressed in the elegant sayings
    of learned men.
If you do not understand and practice these,
Of what use are other studies?

Though an intelligent man knows
     much by himself,
He studies the texts of a learned teacher.
Though precious metal is very fine,
Its value greatly increases after it
     has been cast.

Though there be many forests,   114
Sandalwood grows only in rare places.
Though there be many learned men,
Elegant sayings are seldom found.

The qualities of gold and silver are seen when
     they are melted.
An elephant's goodness appears when he
     enters the field of battle.
A learned man may be judged
By his composition of elegant sayings.

He that is acquainted with the
     manners of the world
Will exercise true religion.
He that practices virtue
Is the living biography of a saint.

Other Dharma Publishing Books

The Voice of the Buddha: The Beauty of Compassion. Complete translation of the Lalitavistara Sūtra, the Buddha's own account of his life, enlightenment, and early teachings.

The Dhammapada. A fresh translation of a traditional collection of the Buddha's essential teachings on 26 subjects, including the nature of mind, self, desire, ignorance, and the path of liberating knowledge.

The Marvelous Companion: Āryaśūra's Jātakamālā. 35 accounts of the Buddha's previous lives, retold by a great Mahāyāna master and poet. Enjoyable for children and adults alike.

Gesture of Balance: A Guide to Self-Healing, Awareness, and Meditation, by Tarthang Tulku. Techniques and attitudes for self-evaluation, growth, and change.

Kum Nye Relaxation, by Tarthang Tulku (2 vols.). 115 clearly-explained, illustrated exercises for integrating the energies of body and mind, deepening relaxation, and increasing concentration.

Time, Space, and Knowledge: A New Vision of Reality. A path-breaking synthesis of philosophic, scientific, and psychological approaches to understanding self and world. With 35 thought experiments that open liberating new perspectives.

Love of Knowledge, by Tarthang Tulku. An independent inquiry into what freezes our thinking, knowledge, and experience into repetitive, enervating patterns. A bridge to the vision expressed in *Time, Space, and Knowledge.*

Crystal Mirror Series, edited by Tarthang Tulku. Introductions to the meaning of Buddha, Dharma, and Sangha, with clear surveys of the view, paths, and history of the Buddhist traditions.

If you order Dharma books directly from the publisher, it will help us to make more such books available. Write for our catalogue of more than fifty titles, illustrated with full-color thanka reproductions.

Dharma Publishing   2425 Hillside Avenue
Berkeley, California 94704 USA